Toys I play with

Noisy toys, Messy toys

Barbara Hunter

www.heinemann.co.uk/library
Visit our website to find out more information about **Heinemann Library** books.

To order:

☎ Phone 44 (0) 1865 888066
Send a fax to 44 (0) 1865 314091
Visit the Heinemann Bookshop at www.heinemann.co.uk/library to browse our catalogue and order online.

First published in Great Britain by Heinemann Library, Halley Court, Jordan Hill, Oxford OX2 8EJ, part of Harcourt Education.
Heinemann is a registered trademark of Harcourt Education Ltd.

Editorial: Jilly Attwood and Claire Throp
Design: Jo Hinton-Malivoire and bigtop, Bicester, UK
Models made by: Jo Brooker
Picture Research: Catherine Bevan
Production: Lorraine Warner

Originated by Dot Gradations
Printed and bound in China by South China Printing Company

ISBN 0 431 16343 X (hardback)
06 05 04 03 02
10 9 8 7 6 5 4 3 2 1

ISBN 0 431 16348 0 (paperback)
06 05 04 03 02
10 9 8 7 6 5 4 3 2 1

British Library Cataloguing in Publication Data
Hunter, Barbara
Noisy/messy toys. – (Toys I play with)
790.1'33
A full catalogue record for this book is available from the British Library.

Acknowledgements
The publishers would like to thank the following for permission to reproduce photographs: Gareth Boden.

Cover photograph reproduced with permission of Gareth Boden.

The publishers would like to thank Annie Davy for her assistance in the preparation of this book.

Every effort has been made to contact copyright holders of any material reproduced in this book. Any omissions will be rectified in subsequent printings if notice is given to the publishers.

Contents

Talking toys

This fluffy teddy bear talks quietly.

This plastic robot talks with a very **loud** voice!

NOISY

Finger painting

How does the paint feel on your hands?

messy

Cars and other vehicles

What noise does a car make?

How do these vehicles sound?

Clay modelling

You can make models out of clay.

What does it feel like when the clay squishes through your fingers?

Telephone

This plastic phone is just like a real one.

'bring' 'bring'

NOISY

Cardboard models

You need lots of glue to stick a cardboard castle together.

Glue sticks to lots of things, especially your **hands**!

Computer games

The computer tells you how to play – it can make funny noises too!

NOISY

Water wheels

You can get very wet when you play with a water wheel.

Do you wear a waterproof apron?

Rattles and whistles

Rattles and whistles are really noisy!

trrr! trrr!
toot! toot!

Touching and hearing

'bring'
'bring'
splashing

Index

Notes for adults

This series supports the young child's knowledge and understanding of their world. The following Early Learning Goals are relevant to the series.

- Find out about, and identify, some features of living things, objects and events that they observe.
- Exploration and investigation: feeling textures and materials.

The series explores a range of different play experiences by looking at features of different toys, the noises they make, or the noises children make when playing with them. The child is encouraged to think about what the noise indicates and whether the noises are loud or quiet. The toys in **Noisy Toys, Messy Toys** are made of a variety of materials including fabric, plastic, wood, metal and glass. 'Messy' play includes the use of other types of material: clay, water, paint and glue. It is important to note that the concepts of 'noisy' and 'messy' are not used in a negative sense but as a way of describing characteristics of toys.

There is an opportunity for the child to compare and contrast the different kinds of play as well as relating them to their own experiences, e.g. some children may find loud noises intimidating and others may dislike the feel of some of the messy activities. While reading the book, the child may enjoy making the noises suggested or go on to create their own noises. Similarly, they may be encouraged to try some of the messy activities shown in the book.

Follow-up activities

By making direct reference to the book the child can be encouraged to try new experiences, e.g. finding all their toys that make a noise. Drawing pictures and adding 'noise bubbles' would be an excellent way for the child to start making their own book.